How to Answer Questions at Your Deposition

Don't let the Gobbledygook Bamboozle You

By

David Grappo

TABLE OF CONTENTS

Chapter 1.   PRELIMINARY CONSIDERATIONS . . . 1

INTRODUCTION
THE ROLE OF THE PLAYERS
    The deposing attorney
    Your attorney
    You
IMAGING - VISUALIZATION
PREPARING OR NOT PREPARING FOR YOUR DEPOSITION
REHEARSALS - PRACTICING YOUR TESTIMONY
HOW TO DRESS FOR YOUR DEPOSITION
WHO WILL ATTEND YOUR DEPOSITION
INTERPRETERS
GETTING TO THE DEPOSITION/TALKING ABOUT IT
WHAT SHOULD YOU BRING TO YOUR DEPOSITION?
STARTING THE DEPOSITION: THE OATH
STARTING THE DEPOSITION: THE ADMONITIONS
STARTING THE DEPOSITION: BACKGROUND QUESTIONS
GENERAL DEMEANOR: KEEP THE RECORD CLEAN
GENERAL DEMEANOR: GETTING "ON THE RECORD"
READING BACK THE RECORD
AVOIDING DISTRACTIONS: WATCHING THE REPORTER
COPING WITH ANNOYING, RUDE, OR ABUSIVE CONDUCT

Chapter 2.   ANSWERING THE QUESTIONS: THE RULES . . 10

TELL THE TRUTH
SAY ONLY WHAT YOU KNOW - BUT WHAT DO YOU KNOW?
    Percipient/firsthand knowledge
    Hearsay
    Estimate/guess
    Opinion
    Speculation

BE BRIEF: VOLUNTEER NOTHING
THE BIG 5 SIMPLE ANSWERS
EXAGGERATION: OVERSTATEMENT AND UNDERSTATEMENT

SUMMARIZE WHEN ANSWERING OPEN-ENDED QUESTIONS
PAUSE TO THINK BEFORE SPEAKING.
TESTIFYING ABOUT DOCUMENTS
TESTIFYING ABOUT CONVERSATIONS
TESTIFYING ABOUT OBSERVATIONS
FLASH RECALL
"ANYTHING ELSE" QUESTIONS
DO NOT VOLUNTEER OTHER SOURCES OF INFORMATION
EVASIVE ANSWERS: IGNORING THE QUESTION
DO NOT EXPLAIN WHY YOU REMEMBER AN EVENT
DO NOT ASSIST THE CONFUSED EXAMINER
PUTTING WORDS IN YOUR MOUTH: LEADING QUESTIONS
PUTTING WORDS IN YOUR MOUTH: SUMMARIZING Q's
DEALING WITH CONFUSING QUESTIONS
    THE GIBBERISH QUESTION
    MULTIPLE NEGATIVES
    COMPOUND QUESTIONS
    LOADED QUESTIONS WITH BUILT-IN ASSUMPTIONS
    THE LONG QUESTION: THE "NICKEL AND DIME" RULE
STATEMENTS AND SPEECHES AS QUESTIONS
INTERRUPTIONS
    The opposing attorney
    Your attorney
    The reporter
"OFF THE RECORD"
MISSTATEMENTS AND INCONSISTENCIES
BREAKS
QUESTIONS BY YOUR ATTORNEY
REVIEW/SIGNING THE DEPOSITION

Chapter 3. FINAL CONSIDERATIONS 28

COMPARING TRIAL AND DEPOSITION TESTIMONY
BREAKING THESE RULES
FORGETTING THESE RULES

APPENDIX: A True/False Self-Test 30

* * *

Chapter 1. PRELIMINARY CONSIDERATIONS

INTRODUCTION

Hollywood has created a fearsome image of trial lawyers. Whether at trial or at a deposition, the relentless lawyer forces the cowering witness to confess to all manner of horrible misdeeds. The lawyer uses words like swords; in this duel the lawyer is destined to win. In Hollywood, attorneys are awesome. If the real life witness feels apprehensive about being deposed, Hollywood has made this feeling understandable.

Fortunately, there are ways to prepare yourself for your deposition in a civil lawsuit. This guide assumes that you are a party to a lawsuit and not an expert witness. This guide also assumes that you have an attorney. If you don't have one, get one. That is your most important first step. This guide will point out numerous ways your attorney can help you at your deposition. It will also show you ways to help yourself.

This manual will not encourage you to give smart, snappy responses to bullying attorneys. A witness should avoid repartee with the opposing attorney. Instead, this manual will encourage you to give short, simple, accurate answers that minimize the chance that you will say something you later regret.

As you read this manual, you should mark any part that you have a question about. There are extra pages at the end for you to write your questions. Discuss your questions with your attorney. You will better prepare yourself for your deposition if you take an active role in the process.

Most people can read through this manual in about an hour. Read it straight through once to get an overview of the deposition process. Reread it or parts of it as often as you feel necessary in order to be familiar with the process.

THE ROLE OF THE PLAYERS

In order to begin your preparation, you must first understand the role of people attending the deposition.

The deposing attorney: The examining attorney wants to know the facts; but even more importantly, the attorney wants to shape the facts so that they favor the attorney's client. Even if you testify truthfully, the jury may disregard your testimony if it is suspicious of what you say. The examining attorney wants to create that suspicion.

The deposing attorney has a long list of ways to try to discredit your truthful testimony. These include trying to show that: (1) you could not accurately see or hear what you testify to; (2) you do not remember accurately what you saw or heard; (3) you are prejudiced against the opposing party and so won't be truthful; (4) your testimony contradicts other statements you have made or documents you have prepared; (5) your testimony is contradicted by other witnesses or by documents others have prepared.

This list does not exhaust the ways that your truthful testimony can be totally or partially discredited! Remember that the opposing attorney is not your friend, no matter how nice the attorney appears to be. The opposing attorney wants your testimony to seem unbelievable.

Your attorney: Your attorney protects you from unfair or improper tactics the deposing attorney may try to use against you. Your attorney cannot give answers for you, but you may consult privately with your attorney during the deposition if you desire to do so. Don't hesitate to ask for this if you think you need to do so! That is why your attorney is there.

You: Your role as a witness is simple. You must answer questions truthfully and you should follow any instructions your attorney may give you. Your goal at your deposition is also simple. You want to answer the questions as briefly as possible and finish your deposition as soon as possible. Brevity is important because every extra word or sentence you speak may provide an opportunity to find an inconsistency in your testimony.

Your goal is NOT to overwhelm the other side with facts in order to convince them to abandon the case. If no settlement occurs and the case goes to trial, you will then have your chance to tell your whole story to the judge or jury. The message you must accept is simple: DON'T TALK TOO MUCH AT YOUR DEPOSITION.

IMAGING - VISUALIZATION

Some people like to deal with stressful situations by visualizing successfully coping with the situation. If you use this technique, the image you should create is that of you, an adult, trying to explain proper behavior to a stubborn, uncooperative child (the opposing attorney). The child is trying to control you and provoke you. As an adult you know that the child can control or anger you only if you allow the child to do so. As an adult you know that you will control the situation if you remain firm and calm. Imagine that!

PREPARING OR NOT PREPARING FOR YOUR DEPOSITION

Preparing for your deposition usually means reviewing any documents about the case and then meeting with your attorney. Consult your attorney before you review any documents. Your attorney may want to limit what you review. In some cases your attorney may prefer that you review nothing at all and that you rely only upon your memory. Discuss with your attorney the strategy you should follow. Your attorney will advise you.

REHEARSALS - PRACTICING YOUR TESTIMONY

Depending on many factors, you and your attorney may spend time practicing your testimony. It is entirely proper for you to do this. Your oath at your deposition obligates you to tell the truth. Your attorney is entitled to assist you so that your truthful testimony will appear as favorable as possible to you. This may include practice in answering questions you may expect to be asked.

You must spend enough time with your attorney so that you and your attorney believe that you are prepared to testify. The amount of time needed varies with each witness and each case.

Discuss with your attorney any fears or concerns you have about your deposition beforehand. It may not be possible to calm all your fears, but you should be able to minimize the number of unexpected questions.

HOW TO DRESS FOR YOUR DEPOSITION

What you wear says something about you. The opposing attorney evaluates everything about you to try to predict how effective you will be before a judge or jury. The way you dress is sometimes a factor. Discuss this with your attorney if there is anything unusual about your appearance or how you dress. If you intend to give no special message about yourself, wear plain business clothes. If there are no special considerations about how you should dress, follow this rule: dress comfortably but neatly.

WHO WILL ATTEND YOUR DEPOSITION

Each attorney involved in the case may attend the deposition. Every party to the lawsuit may also attend. Usually only the attorneys appear. A court reporter will also attend. The court reporter is not an employee of the court. The reporter's duty is simply to record everything said during the deposition. Some depositions are video taped. This guide does not discuss issues created by video taping of depositions.

INTERPRETERS

If English is not your native language, then you may request an interpreter/translator to assist you. You may request an interpreter even if you have some ability to speak English. If you believe that you will understand the questions better in your own language, you can request a translator. The translator will translate all questions into your native language; you then answer in your native language. The translator will translate your answers into English. The reporter will record only the English questions and English translated answers. If you desire this service, advise your attorney so that arrangements can be made.

GETTING TO THE DEPOSITION/TALKING ABOUT IT

Your deposition will usually be held at the office of an opposing attorney. If possible, arrange to meet your attorney and then go to the deposition together. This avoids the possibility that you might arrive before your attorney and inadvertently talk to someone else about your case. The attorney-client privilege permits you to refuse to answer questions about conversations or written communications with your attorney. However, at the deposition you can be asked about any communications you have had with anyone else about the case.

Depending upon the magnitude of the case, everyone to whom you have spoken may be forced to appear for a deposition to answer questions about what you told them. This includes friends and co-workers! To minimize the chance of this, you should talk about your case only to those who need to know.

Discuss with your attorney about whom you can talk to about the case. The old World War II anti-spy admonition applies here: loose lips sink ships.

WHAT SHOULD YOU BRING TO YOUR DEPOSITION?

Answer: bring nothing - unless your attorney tells you to bring something. The party who asks for your deposition can require that you bring documents or things related to the case. Bring only what your attorney tells you to bring. Generally you should let your attorney carry in whatever you bring. Let your attorney control the handling and review of what you bring. This reduces the chance that you will bring or disclose more than is required.

Also avoid bringing cell phones or any other mobile communication device. If you are addicted to these devices you will inevitably pull them out during breaks. Your attention will be distracted. If you text friends about your deposition, you may be very embarrassed to learn that the opposing attorney may now be entitled to examine your text records or depose the people with whom you communicated. Avoid these problems. Just don't bring anything to the deposition that may distract you.

STARTING THE DEPOSITION: THE OATH

Your deposition begins with your oath to tell the truth. The reporter will ask you to raise your right hand and ask you essentially the following question: Do you solemnly swear to tell the truth, the whole truth, and nothing but the truth? You must answer affirmatively before the deposition can begin. Let your attorney know if there is any religious or other reason why you object to taking an oath. The oath can be modified to fit your requirements; but some form of affirmation that you will tell the truth is required. From that time until the conclusion of the deposition, you must speak truthfully.

STARTING THE DEPOSITION: THE ADMONITIONS

A common ritual at depositions is for the deposing attorney to start by asking the "admonition" questions. These questions are designed to see if the witness understands what a deposition is all about and to ascertain the health and readiness of the witness to testify. The questions often seem designed to put you to sleep, humiliate you, or to get you into the habit of answering "yes" to whatever the deposing attorney asks you. This process usually lasts from 2 to 10 minutes. The time varies because attorneys don't agree on what questions need to be asked. The only useful "admonition" question is simply this: Are you ready to start your deposition? Once you answer that question affirmatively, everything else becomes (to quote an amusing legalism) redundantly duplicative.

Most attorneys can recite catechism-like reasons for asking admonition questions. But you will surely never meet an attorney who knows of an example where these preliminary questions ever affected a case. Experience tells us that the admonition questions are a waste of time. Expect them anyway. Tradition trumps experience.

One improper use of "admonitions" is to induce you to agree to something that you need not agree to. A common and seemingly innocuous example is:

QUESTIONER: "If you answer a question I ask, then I will assume that you understand the question, okay?"

You do not need to agree to this. You may misunderstand a question for many reasons. Even if you answer, that does not always mean that you understood the question. You are sworn to tell the truth and that is your obligation to the questioner. Any agreements or deals about the deposition process should be made only through your attorney.

STARTING THE DEPOSITION: BACKGROUND QUESTIONS

After the admonition questions are finished, the questioner usually begins a series of background questions about you. The length of this inquiry will vary depending upon the issues in the case and the importance of your testimony in the case. The questions may be wide ranging and include any of the following about you:

*your name and any previous names you have used
*address and previous addresses
*marital and family history and present status
*educational history
*employment history/military service history
*medical and health history
*income history
*arrest, criminal conviction and imprisonment history
*previous lawsuits as a party sued or suing
*previous testimony in trials or depositions
*previous jury duty
*licenses and professional memberships
*honors or awards received
*social club memberships including internet sites

*hobbies
*materials published
*your relationship to any other party or witness in the case
*any materials you reviewed to prepare for the deposition
*names of any persons you have spoken to about the case
*just about anything else about you that may be relevant.

You must discuss with your attorney in advance anything about you that you would prefer not to discuss at your deposition. You must also advise your attorney of anything important about you or the case that your attorney may not be aware of.

GENERAL DEMEANOR: KEEP THE RECORD CLEAN

Your testimony may someday be read to a judge or jury. You want the judge or jury to think well of you. Be polite, in spite of what anyone is doing to provoke you. Avoid levity, sarcasm, anger, profanity, or any strong language or emotion. Play it straight. Keep it clean. Be serious. A bit of nervousness is natural and okay. It won't show on the transcript.

GENERAL DEMEANOR: GETTING "ON THE RECORD"

Do not nod your head for "yes" or "no" or "I don't know" answers. The court reporter types only the words spoken. Gestures, movements or conduct do not appear in the official transcript. Speak up to get "on the record."

READING BACK THE RECORD

In order to remind everyone of what has been said or asked, the attorneys may occasionally ask the reporter to "read back" a short portion of the transcript. The reporter will comply with the request.

AVOIDING DISTRACTIONS: WATCHING THE REPORTER

Should you look at the examiner during the deposition? This is a matter of your personal conversational style. The printed transcript of your testimony is given greater weight than anyone's differing memory of what may have been said. Even court reporters make errors. You want the transcript to be accurate. Fast paced depositions may generate misquotes of your testimony.

You can help insure accuracy by watching the court reporter and waiting until the reporter finishes typing a question before you answer it. You are less likely to be distracted by other things if you watch the reporter. It is not considered rude if you decide not to look at the examiner during the deposition. Do whatever helps you to focus on the question and to answer it truthfully.

COPING WITH ANNOYING, RUDE, OR ABUSIVE CONDUCT

The deposing attorney's right to use your deposition testimony against you may be compromised if the conditions at the deposition impair your ability to concentrate. In order for you to concentrate and think, you are entitled to an atmosphere without distractions, harassment or intimidation.

Offensive conduct sometimes occurs at depositions. Distractions can be simple noises such as finger tapping, or people wandering in and out and around the room. Ask to consult with your attorney in private if anything occurs which you think is inappropriate and affects your ability to concentrate.

In combating offensive conduct you must first remember that the court reporter types only what is said at the deposition. You or your attorney must therefore speak up and describe whatever the offending person is doing. The reporter will type the verbal picture into the record. This will effectively deter the conduct in almost all cases. If the conduct persists, you or your attorney should continue to state that fact. You may also need to state your opinion as to whether the conduct affects your ability to pay attention to the questions and to give proper responses. In extreme cases, you may need to preface every response you give with your complaint and a threat to leave. In very rare cases, you may need to leave the deposition.

The courts can impose sanctions for misconduct occurring at a deposition. Your attorney should clearly establish any misconduct "on the record" before doing anything drastic, like leaving or threatening to leave.

Chapter 2. ANSWERING THE QUESTIONS: THE RULES

All of history's accumulated wisdom on answering questions at depositions boils down to two rules: (1) tell the truth, (2) but be brief. These two maxims are sometimes helpfully restated as follows: (1) say only what you know, (2) but volunteer nothing. Either formulation gives you the two fundamental principles for answering questions at a deposition. In the excitement and tension of a deposition, you may forget everything else in this manual, but if you follow these two rules you will still do well. A discussion of each of these rules follows.

TELL THE TRUTH

We all know people who have no qualms about misstating or "shading" the truth. Don't do this at your deposition. The reasons follow.

1. All major ethical and moral philosophies in the world urge honesty as the proper policy. Hopefully you are in tune with the majority of great thinkers who have written at length on this subject.

2. Perjury is the deliberate giving of false testimony while under oath. It is a very serious crime.

3. The opposing attorney's job is to ferret out any lies you may tell in order to destroy your credibility. Lawyers have the mystique of being able to smell a lie from a mile away. Telling lies to lawyers is like diving into shark-infested waters with oozing wounds. You may survive, but you invite an attack by someone who will enjoy eating you up. Few thrills excite a trial lawyer like the chance to expose a liar. Don't feed the sharks!

A famous story is told about Abraham Lincoln when he was a trial lawyer. Mr. Lincoln's client was on trial for murder. Mr. Lincoln was interrogating a man who was the only known witness to the murder. The murder occurred in the rural countryside in the middle of the night. The witness claimed to be several dozen yards away from the scene of the crime.

Mr. Lincoln asked the witness how he could be sure of the identity of the killer. The witness confidently answered that he could see the killer by the light of the moon. Mr. Lincoln then went to his briefcase and pulled out his Farmer's Almanac. The Almanac reported that the night in question was moonless. Mr. Lincoln's client was acquitted.

The lesson is simple: don't think you can outwit lawyers by telling lies. You never know what evidence they may pull out of their briefcases. If you challenge the lawyer mystique, you too may become a famous example of why it exists.

4. Jurors are not dumb. Even if the opposing lawyer cannot decisively prove that you have lied, if the jurors believe you are lying about any small thing, then they may disregard <u>all</u> of your testimony as if it were all lies.

5. The penalty for lying can be grossly disproportionate to the seriousness of the lie. History's greatest example of this truth is Richard Nixon who lost the presidency for being dishonest about what he learned about the Watergate burglary. Even if the truth hurts, that hurt is better than the pain that a lie can inflict on you. Cut your losses; lies can multiply them.

6. None of us are saints. The temptation to lie or stretch the truth can strike anyone. Talk to your lawyer about anything you may be tempted to lie about. You may find that the facts that you thought would hurt your case really have no legal impact at all, or that their impact can effectively be minimized. Discuss possible weaknesses in your case with your lawyer in advance. Let your lawyer show you how to present bad facts in the best light. Trust your lawyer. Avoid temptation. Don't tell lies.

7. Your memory is fickle and fallible. Each time you tell the story about something you saw or did, you make small changes in the story. You will often err in describing what you saw. In almost every case your trial and deposition testimony will vary, even if in only subtle ways. A trial lawyer looks for these changes in your story. These changes may be used against you as if you are fabricating everything, or as if you simply don't know what you are talking about. Trial attorneys make mountains out of molehills. Your attorney has enough work to do just fending off attacks on you due to normal lapses in your memory. You can make your attorney's job hopeless if you add deliberate lies on top of that.

SAY ONLY WHAT YOU KNOW-BUT WHAT DO YOU KNOW?

You can only testify about what you know. Attorneys divide your knowledge into general categories. The main categories are:

Percipient/firsthand knowledge includes all things you have directly perceived by hearing, sight, smell, taste, or touch. Percipient facts are anything you perceive with your five senses. You normally testify only to what you have perceived.

Hearsay includes any facts you know from another source such as someone telling you or something you read about. You may testify about your hearsay knowledge at a deposition, but usually not at trial.

Estimate/guess is a fact you believe exists or an opinion you hold based on related knowledge or recollection you have. You are usually allowed to testify to estimates, especially when you are asked about events you witnessed such as the speed of a car.

Opinion is your interpretation of the meaning of facts. You may testify about your opinions at a deposition, but you usually are not allowed to do so at trial because the jury is expected to form its own opinion from the facts. Whether a driver was driving safely or not is something you could testify to at a deposition, but usually not at a trial. At trial you could testify to what you saw the driver doing (weaving, etc.). But the jury would decide whether that was driving safely or not under the circumstances.

Speculation is a fact you believe or an opinion you hold based upon inadequate knowledge or recollection of an event. Speculation is always improper even when asked for. You may advise the questioner if you think the only answer you can give to a question would be speculation. The questioner will then usually withdraw the question.

These categories overlap. Each category has different legal effects. The outcome of the case may depend upon which category your testimony falls into. Attorneys will therefore argue at length about which category your testimony belongs in.

BE BRIEF: VOLUNTEER NOTHING

A deposition is not the chance for you to sell your story to the other side. A deposition is a chance for the other side to poke as many holes as possible in your story. Nothing you can say at your deposition will convince the other side to give up. That is not the purpose of a deposition. Anything you say that is not responsive to the examiner's question may provide an opportunity to discredit your testimony. Each extra sentence and word you speak is an opportunity for you to make a mistake. You must be truthful; but try to be brief.

Another reason for being brief is that you will save time and money. You save money two ways. Your attorney may be paid by the hour. Shorter depositions means lower attorneys' fees. The court reporter gets paid by the number of pages in the transcript. This means that the court reporter is effectively paid by the word! Fewer words means lower costs. Finally, if you are brief, you will also save your own time because the deposition will end sooner.

The essence of being brief is best understood by analyzing how to answer the following question:

"Can you tell me the time?"

In normal conversation, your natural response to this question is to give the questioner the time of day. That is the <u>wrong</u> answer in a deposition. In a deposition the correct response is either "yes" or "no", depending upon whether you know the time of day. In a deposition, you should then <u>stop talking</u> because you have answered the question. If the questioner wants to know the time of day, then wait for <u>that</u> question to be asked. (Warning - do not practice these deposition techniques on your spouse - or you will end up divorced.)

THE BIG 5 SIMPLE ANSWERS

Simple short answers should be used whenever possible. The 5 most important short answers are:

Yes.
No.
I don't know.
I don't recall.
Maybe/sometimes - or similar indefinite answers.

Try to be accurate when using "I don't know" and "I don't recall." "I don't know" can often be used instead of "I don't recall." However, it is better to use "I don't know" only when you never knew the answer. Use "I don't recall" when you have forgotten what you previously knew.

Example: Who was at the meeting?

If you weren't at the meeting, your answer is "I don't know." If you were at the meeting, but can't recall who also attended, use "I don't recall" even though "I don't know" could also apply.

Many people can be embarrassed into trying to answer a question about an event when they have forgotten or didn't really notice what actually occurred. Do not let shame or embarrassment tempt you to say something that you do not recall. Overstretching your memory can easily cause you to make a false statement that the examiner may then pounce on. <u>Stick with "I don't recall" or "I don't know" unless you are certain of your answer.</u> On the other hand, you must not let the examiner coax you or bully you into saying you do not recall an event just because your memory is hazy about other parts of it.

Sometimes your answer to a question will be an indefinite response such as "maybe", or "sometimes", or "not always." In normal conversation you usually then go on to explain why your response is indefinite. Do not give the explanation unless asked to do so. Volunteer nothing.

Avoid diluting short answers with tag-on qualifiers such as:
"Yes, *I think so*"
"No, *probably not*"
"I don't know *for sure*"
"I don't remember *right now*"

Such qualifiers invite follow-up questions about why you have qualified your answer. If you think you must dilute one of the Big Five

Simple Answers, then you probably need to rethink your answer. Take more time to think in order to give an answer that does not have the tag-on qualifier.

EXAGGERATION: OVERSTATEMENT AND UNDERSTATEMENT

Any form of exaggeration is just as bad as a false statement. It casts doubt on the truth of anything else you may say. Don't overstate or understate a fact. Strive for simple accuracy. Say only what you know.

SUMMARIZE WHEN ANSWERING OPEN-ENDED QUESTIONS

Open-ended questions are those that potentially require long answers. Questions asking for what, why or how are usually open-ended type questions. Questions asking for who, when, or where usually are not open-ended, but may still require long answers. When possible, give short summary answers to all questions.

For example, on a particular night you may have done the following: you met friends after work; you went with them to a restaurant for dinner; then you all went to a theater to see a movie; then some of you went to an ice cream parlor for some dessert, and then a few of you went to a late night bowling alley for a few games; then you went home. If the questioner asks you what you did that night after work, you could respond with a long explanation of everything you did. You could also give a short summary answer as follows:

RESPONSE: "I went out."

Note that the long explanation and the short summary are both 100% responsive to the question and both are 100% true. But the long explanation violates the "be brief - volunteer nothing" rule. Give summary answers whenever you can. Let the examiner ask follow-up questions for whatever detail is desired. If your summary is accepted without any follow-ups, then you have shortened your deposition.

It may take you several moments or minutes to think of a proper summary answer. Take all the time you need.

PAUSE TO THINK BEFORE SPEAKING.

A short accurate answer may take longer to prepare than a long answer. Stories are told about witnesses who thought silently for several minutes before answering a difficult question. If you need a long time to think about your answer, take it. The pace of a deposition is the only part of a deposition that you can control. You must slow the pace to whatever is comfortable for you. You must not let the opposing attorney rush you if that may cause you to make a mistake.

TESTIFYING ABOUT DOCUMENTS

Many depositions revolve around identifying documents and explaining the information contained in them. The questioner may ask you questions about the documents before showing them to you. This is proper in order to see how much you recall without reading the document. If you cannot answer a question without looking at the document, then your proper response is simply "I don't know" or "I don't recall." After exhausting your memory, the examiner may let you see the document in order to refresh your memory and to ask you more questions.

Any attorney may ask the reporter to "mark" a document. That means that a copy of the document will be attached to the deposition transcript. Each marked document is given an identifying number or letter.

TESTIFYING ABOUT CONVERSATIONS

You will frequently be asked to testify about conversations. This may include where and when held, who participated, and most importantly, what was said. You may not remember exactly what was said in a conversation. If asked, tell the examiner only what you recall. Do not summarize or paraphrase the conversation until asked to do so. You will probably be asked to do so. A typical exchange in a deposition may go like this:

QUESTIONER: Do you remember having a conversation with Mr. X?
RESPONSE: Yes.
QUESTIONER: Tell me what was said in the conversation.

RESPONSE: I don't recall the exact words spoken.
QUESTIONER: Can you tell me in general what the conversation was about?
RESPONSE: Yes.
QUESTIONER: Tell me in general what the conversation was about.

TESTIFYING ABOUT OBSERVATIONS

Your deposition may be taken because you saw something happen - such as an automobile accident. You may have no connection to the lawsuit other than that you witnessed something happen. In these situations you may not have your own attorney, but an attorney in the case may volunteer to represent you if your expected testimony favors his or her client.

Even when you have no financial interest in the case the questioning may seem hostile to you. This is because the attorney who does not like what you say will try to find a way to discredit your testimony. You should still follow the basic rules: be truthful and be brief.

FLASH RECALL

Long after answering a question you may remember something that you should have said. Keep these flash recollections to yourself until you have had an opportunity to speak to your attorney. Ask for a private conference. Let your attorney advise you as to when and how to correct your testimony.

"ANYTHING ELSE" QUESTIONS

In order to be sure that you have stated all that you know about an important event or conversation, most attorneys will continue to ask you "is there anything else you recall" about that event. Eventually, your memory will be exhausted. At that point, don't let the examiner box you into a statement that nothing else was said or done at the event. Simply say that is all you can recall. This allows for the possibility that you will have a "flash recall" later.

The "anything else" question may be asked in different ways. The examiner may ask you: Can you tell me anything else about (that event)?

Your response to this form of the question should be something like: I will try to answer any specific question you ask of me.

The "anything else" question might be asked this way: Is there anything else you want to tell me about (that event)? Here the questioner is trying to get you to talk to see if you will say something carelessly when no specific question has been asked. There is nothing you should want to say to the questioner. Simply reply "no" to the question. Remember the rule: volunteer nothing.

DO NOT VOLUNTEER OTHER SOURCES OF INFORMATION

If you cannot answer a question unless you refer to other sources of information, simply state that you cannot answer the question. Do not volunteer what information you need or where you could get it. Never identify other persons who might have information unless specifically asked to do so. Except as discussed below, don't hint that you could get other information by qualified answers such as: "I don't know right now" or "I can't tell you from memory." If you don't know, simply say: "I don't know." Then wait for the next question.

Sometimes you will be able to answer a question only because someone else gave you the information. This is hearsay knowledge, not percipient knowledge. It is risky to give an answer based upon hearsay knowledge unless you are certain the hearsay is true or unless you alert the questioner that your knowledge is hearsay. This is because your hearsay information may be erroneous. Your credibility may be questioned if you gave the impression that your answer was from your firsthand knowledge. On the other hand, an "I don't know" answer might not be appropriate because of the hearsay information you have.

Example: Who was at the meeting?

If you were not at the meeting and are not sure if your hearsay information is correct, you could give a qualified answer such as:

RESPONSE: I don't have any firsthand knowledge of that.

This response is a slight evasion of the question, but it would be a 100% true statement for you to make. This response gives a hint to the examiner to ask follow up questions about what you may or may not know. Wait for the follow up questions. You may or may not get one.

EVASIVE ANSWERS: IGNORING THE QUESTION

Politicians are masters of this technique: A television reporter asks the politician a tough question. The politician ignores the question and gives a short speech about something that may not even be related to what was asked. The reporter thanks the politician and has already forgotten what he asked about.

Don't expect this technique to work well for you at your deposition. Experienced attorneys may interpret your evasiveness as an attempt to hide unfavorable facts. Expect persistence in response to evasiveness.

Evasive answers also violate the "volunteer nothing" rule. Anything you say that is not responsive to the question is volunteered information. Avoid evasive answers; but see the limited exception in the preceding section when your only knowledge is based on hearsay information.

A final reason for avoiding evasive answers is that they make you appear to be evasive! Judges, juries, and attorneys get suspicious of evasive people. You will occasionally misunderstand a question and give an unintentional evasive answer. Don't compound this by deliberately giving evasive answers.

DO NOT EXPLAIN WHY YOU REMEMBER AN EVENT

Ironically, it can be harmful when you remember too much detail about an event. It may appear that you are fabricating everything. There may be a special reason why you remember an event in unusual detail. Don't disclose that reason unless you are asked to do so. Let your attorney know later if there is such a reason. Your attorney will see that you get an opportunity to explain that reason at trial, if it is necessary to do so.

DO NOT ASSIST THE CONFUSED EXAMINER

The examiner's questions may be nonsensical because the examiner does not understand words used in your occupation or because the examiner does not understand something else about you. If you notice this happening, ask for a private conference with your attorney before answering. Your attorney may or may not want you to clear up the misunderstanding. Let your attorney help you decide what to do.

PUTTING WORDS IN YOUR MOUTH: LEADING QUESTIONS

Leading questions are any questions in which you are asked to affirm or deny a version of the facts. This is sometimes called "putting words in your mouth" because the questioner tells the story; you just affirm or deny it. Example:

QUESTIONER: Isn't it true that you drove straight to work from your home this morning?
RESPONSE: Yes.

This form of question is proper for the examiner to ask. Answer these questions if you can with a simple answer such as: yes, no, I don't know, I don't recall, maybe, etc. But be on guard because the questioner's version of the case is not the same as yours. Slight changes in the question may change your answer.

PUTTING WORDS IN YOUR MOUTH: SUMMARIZING Q'S

A summarizing question is a type of leading question in which the questioner rephrases your testimony and asks you if you agree with the rephrasing. The rephrasing will often have a new twist on it with which you do not agree. Be careful when answering this type of question. Be sure you agree with every part of the questioner's summary.

Attorneys often abuse this questioning technique. The questioner may try to summarize large portions of your testimony and misstate important parts when doing so. The length and convoluted nature of the question may make it hard to pinpoint all of the ways that the summary is inaccurate. You need not restate every portion of your testimony if you simply deny that the questioner's summary is accurate.

The examiner may then ask you to pinpoint the inaccurate parts of the examiner's question. If you can do so easily, then do so. But you need not explain each error in the examiner's convoluted misstatement of your testimony. That is not the purpose of a deposition. If the question was too lengthy or convoluted for you to easily answer or explain, then say so. You may ask the questioner to rephrase the summary question so that you can easily understand it, analyze it, and answer it.

DEALING WITH CONFUSING QUESTIONS

As a witness you are entitled to refuse to answer questions that you do not understand. For many reasons, lawyers have a tendency to ask confusing questions. A sampling of five different types of confusing questions and how to deal with them follows.

THE GIBBERISH QUESTION: Attorneys are highly educated, but they trip over the English language just like everyone else. If you hear a question that you don't understand, say so. Don't let the gobbledygook bamboozle you!

Example: How did critical mass affect the tipping point in strategizing your priorities?
RESPONSE: I don't understand your question.

You must not answer any question you do not understand. You may ask that a question be repeated or rephrased if that would help you.

MULTIPLE NEGATIVES: Many attorneys are indirect or evasive in speaking. These attorneys often lace their questions with multiple negatives. Ask for the question to be restated if it confuses you.

Example: Do you deny that you don't categorically oppose the conclusions rejected in this report?
RESPONSE: Can you rephrase that question and simplify it for me?
QUESTIONER: Oh, okay. Do you agree with what is said in this report?

COMPOUND QUESTIONS: A compound question is really two or more questions combined into one. These questions are improper and often occur through carelessness by the questioner.

Example: Tell me who you work for and what you do.

If your attorney does not object to this question, you have several options:

   *Answer both questions.
   *Ask the questioner which question you should answer first and answer only that question. Wait to see if the second question gets asked again.
   *Ask the questioner to repeat the question because you heard more than one question and you don't know which one to answer.

The latter two approaches are most consistent with the "volunteer nothing" rule.

LOADED QUESTIONS WITH BUILT-IN ASSUMPTIONS:
The most famous loaded question (those with a built-in assumption) is "When did you stop beating your wife?" You have sufficiently answered such a question if you simply deny that you beat your spouse.

Modern versions of the classic question tack-on offensive elements to an otherwise innocent question.

Example: Isn't it true that you drove straight to work from home this morning after abandoning your starving children?

You need not answer such a question. You can simply say that you do not agree with the assumptions stated in the question. Then wait for the examiner's next question. If you answer the innocent part of the question, you must still make clear that you do not agree with the tacked-on assumptions.

Example: I did not leave my children starving at home, but I did drive straight to work from home this morning.

It is usually safer not to answer this type of question at all. Simply say that you do not agree with the assumptions in the question. Any answer you give will probably violate the volunteer nothing rule. You can ask the examiner to break down the question into its various parts so that you can easily identify those parts that are true from those which are not.

THE LONG QUESTION: THE "NICKEL AND DIME" RULE:
Some attorneys just seem to enjoy listening to themselves. Their questions show it by their length. Use the unofficial "nickel and dime" or "5 and 10" rule to measure objectionable length:

*Any question that takes more than 10 seconds to ask is almost always too long. You can ask the questioner to simplify it.
*Questions that are too long are usually objectionable because they are gibberish, compound, contain built-in assumptions and/or multiple negatives.
*Any question that takes between 5 and 10 seconds to ask may be too long. Pause and think before you respond.
*Any question that takes less than 5 seconds to ask is not too long. There may be other problems with the question, but it is probably not too long.

The "5 and 10" rule also applies to your answers. If you think that your answer to a question will take more than 5 or 10 seconds, you should pause before answering. Your answers should not normally take that long. Long-winded answers may provide more information than was asked for.

Try to be brief! Summarize. Volunteer nothing.

STATEMENTS AND SPEECHES AS QUESTIONS

Frustrated attorneys sometimes resort to giving long statements or speeches that are often insulting and intended to provoke you. At the end of the speech they turn to you as if it was your turn to say something in reply. If this happens, you need not reply. But if you do, your only reply should be "what is your question?"

Speak only in reply to a proper question. Don't make speeches. Don't let yourself be provoked.

INTERRUPTIONS

Interruptions of your testimony come from three main sources: the opposing attorney, your own attorney, or the reporter. Your response is different for each type of interruption.

<u>The opposing attorney</u>: The examiner should not interrupt your answers with a new question. In order to discourage this conduct your attorney (or you, if your attorney doesn't notice the interruption) should point out the interruption to the examiner. Ask if you can finish your answer to the previous question. After doing so, stop and wait for the next question to be asked.

If the interruption distracts you into forgetting what you were about to say, you can ask that the recorder read back the previous question and your partial reply. That should help reorient you. If the examining attorney habitually interrupts you, ask each time for the previous question and your reply to be read back. That should eventually deter the bad behavior.

<u>Your attorney</u>: Stop speaking when your attorney interrupts. Your attorney probably intends to object to the question. Listen to your attorney's objection. Your attorney is not allowed to tell you what to say, but each objection has that effect anyway. Take the hint if you can. But wait to see if your attorney allows you to answer the question. Sometimes your attorney will object and then "instruct" you not to answer a question. Follow your attorney's advice.

The reporter: Stop speaking whenever the reporter interrupts. The reporter interrupts only when two people speak at once or when one person speaks too fast or not loud enough. You must stop to allow the reporter to record everything. Then, slow down if necessary. After an interruption by the reporter, ask that the reporter read back the last few moments of the transcript in order to be sure that your testimony was accurately recorded.

A safe practice is to watch the reporter during the deposition. Don't start answering a question until you see the reporter finish typing it. This allows you a moment to think about your answer. It also allows your attorney to object to the question if he or she is inclined to do so.

"OFF THE RECORD"

At any time any attorney may ask to go "off the record." This means that the court reporter will stop typing until the attorney asks to "go back on." Off the record conversations do not appear in the transcript. But when you "go back on" the opposing attorney may ask you questions about conversations that occurred off the record (except private conversations with your attorney). Stay alert, even when "off the record." The sharks are still circling around you. Don't feed them.

MISSTATEMENTS AND INCONSISTENCIES

No matter how certain you are in the truth of your testimony, misstatements and inconsistencies will usually occur.

If the examiner confronts you with an inconsistency in your testimony, do not fear that your case is lost. State, if asked, your present recollection. State, if asked, the reason for any inconsistency if you know it. You may ask to meet privately with your attorney so you can think about your responses. Let your attorney advise you on how to correct your testimony, if that is necessary. Stay calm.

BREAKS

As a witness you are entitled to be reasonably comfortable so that you can think clearly and give accurate answers to the questions. If you want to stop briefly to eat, drink, get fresh air, go to the bathroom, talk privately to your attorney, or for any other reason, just ask for it. If, after a long day of testifying, you are too exhausted to continue, say so. The deposition can be reset to finish on another day.

How long will your deposition last? It could vary from a few minutes, to hours, and even to days. It depends upon how much is at stake and how much you know. Your attorney should be able to give you an estimate.

QUESTIONS BY YOUR ATTORNEY

Your attorney is entitled to ask you questions when the opposing attorney finishes. Usually your attorney will not ask any questions. This is consistent with the volunteer nothing rule. Sometimes, however, your attorney will ask you questions. The most common reason for doing so is to correct or clarify your testimony. If you will not be available for trial, then your attorney may question you so that your entire story will be available at least in transcript form for the trial.

REVIEW/SIGNING THE DEPOSITION

You receive still one more chance to correct errors after the deposition is over. Once the transcript is prepared you are given up to 30 days to review, correct and/or make written changes to your testimony. You will also be asked to sign the final version of the transcript. If you make changes, then both the original version and your corrections become part of the official record. At trial the opposing attorney may ask you about any changes you have made.

You are not required to review, correct or sign your transcript. Some attorneys advise their clients not to correct the transcript or sign it. Discuss this with your attorney.

Chapter 3. FINAL CONSIDERATIONS

COMPARING TRIAL AND DEPOSITION TESTIMONY

Your approach to testifying in a trial will differ from the approach you take at your deposition. That is because you have different objectives. At trial you want your full story to come before the judge or jury. At your deposition you want to say the minimum necessary in order to avoid attacks on your story. These differing goals should never be inconsistent with your duty to tell the truth.

Your opportunity to tell your story at trial will typically be during your attorney's examination of you. You need not be concerned that your deposition focused only on things unfavorable to you. You can tell your whole story at trial.

BREAKING THESE RULES

Following the rules in this guide will not guarantee that you will win your lawsuit. Following these rules is not even an assurance that you will make the best possible presentation of your story. Experience, good judgment and common sense must sometimes override these rules. When there are no other considerations, however, following the rules in this guide will usually be your best course.

Testifying is like storytelling. It is an art, not a science. The only absolutely unbreakable rule is rule number 1: you must tell the truth. All other rules are merely guidelines. You can ignore the guidelines and sometimes you should do so, but you should have a reason for doing so.

FORGETTING THESE RULES

At your deposition you will not remember all that you have learned in this manual. You will make mistakes and violate even the rules you remember. When all else fails you must remember at least the two basic rules for deposition testimony:

1. Tell the truth; say only what you know.
2. Be brief; volunteer nothing.

You can do well with just that much.

*   *   *

APPENDIX

A True/False Self-Test. Answer true or false to each item:

1. Let's suppose you are well known for your wit, charm or take-charge personality. At your deposition you can use the force of your compelling personality to dazzle the opposing attorney into accepting your entire story. True or False?

    Answer: False. Think of the opposing attorney like a hired gun from the Old West days. His job is to destroy you and your story. You can also think of a deposition as like going to a shooting gallery in an arcade. But in this game YOU are the target. Despite your own belief, your story has weaknesses and likely has provable errors. A skilled trial attorney finds those lapses, magnifies them, and uses them against you. Protect yourself by not making yourself a bigger target than necessary. Be brief. Summarize. Volunteer nothing.

2. The opposing attorney seems like a very intelligent person. If you don't quite understand the question asked of you, it must be your fault. In order to avoid appearing to be ignorant, you should try to answer the question you think the attorney is asking. True or False?

    Answer: False. In normal conversation when someone says or asks something that doesn't make sense the conversation usually just continues on as if nothing happened. Don't let that happen in a deposition. Anything you say in response to a question you do not understand is volunteered information. It violates the volunteer nothing rule. If you don't understand a question, you must say so. (Second warning: don't practice these deposition tactics on your spouse or friends. If you do you will end up divorced and friendless.)

3. When you tell the examining attorney that you don't understand his question, he looks insulted and demands to know what it is that you do not understand. You should then give a thorough critical analysis of the question, including grammatical corrections if applicable. True or False?

Answer: False. It is not your duty to fix whatever question the examiner is trying to ask you. Sometimes the problem may be simple such as using a word or technical term you are not familiar with. But for anything more complex than that, you are entitled to simply repeat that you didn't understand the question and let the questioner figure out how to fix it.

4. Cooperation is the soul of civilized society. If you are asked a question that you cannot answer, but know how to find the answer, you should offer to provide that information. True or False?

Answer: False. The volunteer-nothing rule applies here too. If you do not know the answer to a question, just say, "I don't know." If the questioner wants to know if you know where to find the answer, wait for that question. (Third and final warning: do not practice these deposition skills on your spouse, friends or coworkers. If you do you will end up divorced, friendless and ostracized.) You must be truthful at your deposition and you should always be polite, but that does not require that you be helpful or cooperative.

5. If you are asked questions about an event you witnessed, but don't recall some minor details about it, you can just fill in minor details and say what you think probably happened. True or False?

Answer: False. Deposition rule # 1 tells you to say only what you know. What you think probably happened doesn't count. If you don't know something, say so. None of us accurately recall all the details of events we witness. In fact, we almost always remember some things inaccurately. Trial attorneys meticulously go over your trial and deposition testimony to see if they can find the one or more provable inaccuracies in your testimony. They then tell the judge or jury this shows you to be unreliable. The jury may accept that argument. Don't make up stuff. It can be fatal to your case.

6. Practice telling your story about your lawsuit to your friends and coworkers. They will surely be able to offer you helpful suggestions from their own experiences. True or False?

Answer: False. Nearly everyone to whom you have spoken about your lawsuit can be subjected to a deposition to explain what you said. There are few exceptions. Talk to your attorney about whom you can talk to about your lawsuit.

7. Depositions can be simultaneously exhausting and boring. To relieve tension, bring your cell phone and use it during short breaks, lunch breaks, and bathroom breaks. True or False?

Answer: False. When the deposition resumes after a break, you can be asked to explain to whom you communicated and what you said during the break. (Conversations with your attorney are excepted here.) The safest practice is just not to bring any mobile communication devices with you to your deposition.

8. There may be some embarrassing facts about you or about your lawsuit that your attorney is not aware of. If you conceal these facts from your own attorney, you can successfully conceal them from the opposing attorney too. True or False?

Answer: False. There are weaknesses in every story. But surprises are worse than weaknesses. If you are candid with your attorney you may find that your worries can be overcome or not have much effect on your case. If there is a fatal weakness in your case, it is always better to deal with that early on. You don't want your attorney to find out too late that the diligent opposing attorney somehow discovered your secret.

9. Some attorneys bring an "army" of associates, paralegals, files, and related paraphernalia with them to depositions. This show of force is intended to and should intimidate you. True or False?

Answer: False. Some people never grasp the meaning of the variations on the joke: how many people does it take to change a light bulb? A poorly organized effort often requires more manpower than an organized one. As long as the army remains quiet and polite, tolerate it.

10. You now have a greater understanding for what a deposition is all about. You also have a greater appreciation and sympathy for the sentiments expressed in the famous line about lawyers from one of Shakespeare's plays: "The first thing we do, let's kill all the lawyers." True or False?

    Answer: True.

* * *

Made in the USA
Middletown, DE
27 July 2019